Concert and Contest COLLECTION

Compiled and Edited by **H. VOXMAN**

T0071532

for

Eb ALTO SAXOPHONE with piano accompaniment

CONTENTS

RUBANK®

HAL•LEONARD®
CORPORATION
7777 W. BLUEMOUND RD. P.O. BOX 13819 MILWAUKEE, WI 53213

At the Hearth
(Au Foyer)
from Suite Miniature

Eb Alto Saxophone

A. GRETCHANINOFF, Op. 145, No. 8
Transcribed by H. Voxman

Evening Waltz
(Valse dans le Soir)
from Suite Miniature

E♭ Alto Saxophone

A. GRETCHANINOFF, Op. 145, No. 10
Transcribed by H. Voxman

Minuet
from Haffner Music, K. 250

Eb Alto Saxophone

W. A. MOZART
Transcribed by H. Voxman

Mélodie

Eb Alto Saxophone

SIMON POULAIN
Edited by H. Voxman

Canzonetta and Giga

Eb Alto Saxophone

LEROY OSTRANSKY

Sonatina
(Based On Trio V)

Eb Alto Saxophone

J. HAYDN
Transcribed by H. Voxman

Andante and Allegro

Eb Alto Saxophone

ANDRÉ CHAILLEUX
Edited by H. Voxman

Largo and Allegro
from Sonata VI

Eb Alto Saxophone

G. F. HANDEL
Transcribed by H. Voxman

Élégie

Eb Alto Saxophone

J. Ed. BARAT
Edited by H. Voxman

Introduction and Rondo

Eb Alto Saxophone

LEROY OSTRANSKY

Recitative and Allegro

Eb Alto Saxophone

PAUL KOEPKE

Fantaisie Mauresque

Eb Alto Saxophone

F. COMBELLE
Edited by H. Voxman

Concertante

Eb Alto Saxophone

E. PALADILHE
Transcribed by H. Voxman

Eb Alto Saxophone

First Concertino

Eb Alto Saxophone

GEORGES GUILHAUD
Transcribed by H. Voxman

Eb Alto Saxophone